CONSIDERING GETTING A PSYCHIC READING?

While researching her book ***Adventures of a Soul: Psychics, Mediums, the Mystical, and Me***, author Anne Newgarden had nearly a hundred psychic readings and conducted dozens of interviews with psychics and mediums she found to be excellent at what they do. In this short guide, Anne shares behind-the-scenes insights, advice, and "pet peeves" from these top psychics and mediums, based on her own experiences and the sometimes surprising information they shared.

You'll learn . . .

- *The many different types of psychics–including mediums–and the tools they use*
- *How to find a good psychic, and red flags to watch out for*
- *What to expect during a reading, and how to prepare for one*
- *Tips for getting the best guidance and experience possible during your reading*
- *Common mistakes even seasoned clients may make during a reading*
- *And more!*

Whether you're about to have your hundredth reading, are a true beginner considering your first, or are just plain curious about all this "*woo-woo*" stuff, ***15 Things Good Psychics Wished You Knew Before a Reading*** will bring you a deeper understanding of psychics and mediums, and what REALLY happens during a reading.

Praise for Anne Newgarden's

15 THINGS GOOD PSYCHICS WISHED YOU KNEW BEFORE A READING

A great read, and I enjoyed all the useful information, too. Anne has a great way of sharing her experiences, with a wealth of knowledge and humor, that makes this book a joy to read. I highly recommend it to anyone that's looking for a friendly and helpful guide to researching the world of psychics.
—*Lee J., theatrical producer, Mequon, WI*

Much more than its title suggests! This mini book, ***15 Things Good Psychics Wished You Knew Before a Reading,*** is, on its face, about a way to choose a psychic reader, and the mindset, and the questions to ask when getting the reading, and it does an amazing job on that level. Yet, on a deeper level, Anne's book is about a way to live life with an open, not gullible, and an accepting but questioning mind. This book is for those seeking Spiritual growth and is not limited to those who may have a psychic reading. Do yourself the favor of reading and, at varied periods, of rereading this gem!
—***Kevin O., retired attorney, Cuenca, Ecuador***

A fun and informative read for anyone curious about what to expect from their first visit to a psychic. Also helpful for more experienced seekers of supernatural insight, this quick little list lays the groundwork for deeper understanding. Wish this had been available sooner!
—*Amy F., professor, Bradley Beach, NJ*

I thoroughly enjoyed reading this! This little book reveals so many interesting and nuanced points about the world of psychics, all imparted in an intelligent, down-to-earth manner laced with humor and charm. I learned so much and can't wait to read her book ***Adventures of a Soul* . . .**
—*Kim R., painter, Provence, France*

If *Consumer Reports* had an equivalent in the metaphysical world, this would qualify as one of their buying guides. It provides practical, sensible information in Anne Newgarden's delightful voice, honed through (apparently) extensive first-hand experience. I've never had a reading or met with a medium, but I've always been curious. I was pointed in the direction of this guide by someone who dabbles in this stuff; and after reading it, I'm (excuse the expression) psyched to get a reading. Let's see what happens . . .
—*Peter C., writer, Brooklyn, NY*

A wonderful guide and a fun read. Answered so many questions I didn't realize I needed to ask. An insightful and enjoyable guide sure to help make your first or next psychic reading a valued experience. Highly recommended. Wish it was available years ago!
—*Monica A., CPA, Canaan, New Hampshire*

A practical guide to what might be regarded as the impractical. How much more I would have gotten from my past readings had I read Ms. Newgarden's wise and well considered musings and advice. I look forward to reading her book.
—*Jim C., photographer, Copenhagen, Denmark*

A terrific guide for the afterlife-curious. Whether through personal tragedy or philosophical curiosity, many of us find ourselves drawn to the big question of whether there's life after physical death, which in turn probably means we turn to a medium for connection with that other world, or to find answers to our questions. This book is a delightful and insightful guide for those who may be about to embark on this journey, offering insights and tips from mediums themselves. Clearly, Anne has done her homework here, having interviewed many mediums. If you're thinking of working with a medium, this book is an excellent starting point. Highly recommend!
—*Roland J., editorial director, NY, NY*

15 THINGS GOOD PSYCHICS WISHED YOU KNEW

BEFORE A READING

15 THINGS GOOD PSYCHICS WISHED YOU KNEW BEFORE A READING

ANNE NEWGARDEN

Star Garden Press

Copyright © 2022 Anne Newgarden

All rights reserved

The information in this book is true and complete to the best of the author's knowledge. Any advice or recommendations are made without guarantee on the part of the author or publisher. The author and publisher disclaim any liability in connection with the use of this information.

No part of this book may be reproduced, or stored in a retrieval system, or transmitted in any form or by any means, electronic, mechanical, photocopying, recording, or otherwise, without express written permission of the publisher.

Cover design by: M. Dobkins

INTRODUCTION

Greetings, Reader!

While conducting research for my book ***Adventures of a Soul: Psychics, Mediums, the Mystical, and Me***, I had a LOT of psychic readings—nearly a hundred! I concocted an informal experiment: If I had readings with ten different *intuitives*—another word for psychics, and the one most psychics I know actually prefer, though I'll use *psychic* here for familiarity's sake—every six months, over the course of several years, would they end up telling me any of the same things?

Through these many, many readings, and dozens of in-depth interviews with the psychics with whom I worked, I learned a great deal about what it is that psychics feel they're really doing, how they do it, and how it can be helpful—or in some cases, NOT helpful! It's information these psychics *wished their clients knew*, since any good psychic's aim is to give you the best, most helpful reading possible.

And now, Dear Reader, I'm pleased to share it with you, starting with the basics and moving on to some important concepts even those of you who've worked with psychics for years, or decades, might not know. Understanding these concepts changed the way I approach readings, the types of questions I ask, and how I understand and evaluate what the psychic shares. I've also included some advice from these psychics on things they feel are counterproductive during a reading, as well as a few of their specific "pet peeves."

May all your readings to come be fruitful and fulfilling!

1

NO TWO PSYCHICS ARE ALIKE.

PSYCHICS WANT YOU TO KNOW: They come in an infinite variety, and no two are precisely alike in how they receive what they receive, what they feel they can do best, and what they feel they can DO, period. Every psychic has a particular set of skills that they offer. Good psychics want you to understand this, as finding the psychic whose skills fit your needs is crucial to having a helpful and satisfying reading. You wouldn't go to a cardiologist for a torn metatarsal. It's the same with psychics, and they appreciate clients who've taken the time to educate themselves a bit on their many different types of intuitive offerings.

One very popular psychic skill is mediumship. Those who do this often refer to themselves as *psychic mediums*, or simply *mediums*, but many mediums have other types of psychic skills as well. It is often said, "All mediums are psychic, but not all psychics are mediums," and generally my psychics agree—though some feel that precisely what skills a psychic can use is limited only by their own beliefs. In any case, psychic mediums can contact those who have crossed over to the Other Side, or, as one of my favorite mediums fondly refers to them, "dead people." If you want to contact your dear departed grandma or your BFF whose passing left a hole in your heart, be sure to look for a medium, or a psychic who includes mediumship in their skill set.

Some psychics receive information about health. You may have heard the terms *medical medium* or *medical intuitive*, which those who specialize in this skill sometimes use. In my experience, many psychics who *don't* use those terms to label themselves are still awfully accurate with picking up and assessing health issues, and even offering suggestions as to what might or might not help. Other psychics will decidedly not go there, feeling it's too great a responsibility, wary of legal repercussions, or simply because it's something they don't feel they can do. Case in point, this "pet peeve" one psychic medium shared with me: "Women who haven't had a mammogram in years—or *ever*!—who want to know if they're healthy. 'Call a darn doctor, not a psychic!'" she vented. And I do take her point.

Another psychic skill is *animal communication*. Psychics with this ability can communicate with your dog, cat, rabbit, anaconda . . . most any type of animal with whom you have a relationship. This can be handy in solving behavioral problems, and even exposing unseen health issues. One psychic I know had a horse tell her that another horse in an adjacent pen was suffering with a badly cracked, painful hoof. The psychic shared this information with the horse in question's owner and sure enough, when she checked, it was true, and the neighboring horse got some much-needed help. FYI, if you'd like to connect with your long-departed childhood Dalmatian, Fritz, rest assured that many animal psychics can do mediumship, too. And vice versa: Many mediums who don't call themselves animal communicators can contact departed pets.

Some psychics can get information about what are usually referred to as your *past lives*. While past-life regressionists don't have to be psychics—they generally use hypnosis to put the client into a light trance state and then lead them through some exercises designed to connect them with a number of their other incarnations— some psychics can simply pick up information about a client's past lives in a reading. Not all psychics necessarily believe in reincarnation or past lives—as I've pointed out, psychics are a very varied lot, with, for example, different types of religious upbringings that may or may not have influenced their beliefs and preferences. And some may just be inexperienced in looking into past-life stuff. But the majority of the psychics I've worked with have made reference to a belief in past lives, and many have brought in fascinating information about my own during our sessions.

Psychics may have other areas in which they feel they have expertise. Some consider themselves at their best with questions about love and relationships, work and careers, finances, and so on. I've had astounding success asking certain psychics for help with writing projects, titles for my books, and even book-cover art. (Who'd a thunk it?) One amazing psychic I worked with felt her particular gift was to share with clients what their purpose was in this lifetime—they often came to her, she said, when they were not doing what they had come here to do, and sensed that something was "off." (And in my case, she was spot on!)

Psychics also vary in how they receive the information they receive. They may psychically hear things (often termed *clairaudience*, meaning "clear hearing"), see things (*clairvoyance*), feel things (*clairsentience*), taste things (*clairgustance*), smell things (*clairolfaction*), or simply know things (*claircognizance*)—or some combination of the above.

Psychics vary in how they work, too. They may use tarot cards (or even regular old playing cards!), tea leaves, the I Ching, pendulums, crystals or gem stones, palmistry, astrology, or numerology—and may want the date, time, and place of your birth in some cases, depending on their tool or system of choice. Many psychics use the cards or other objects as a sort of "spring-board" to jumpstart their intuition or as a focal point to clear their mind of "noise" that might get in the way of what's psychically coming in. Some psychics receive information from nonphysical beings such as angels, spirit guides, "masters," extraterrestrial beings, and even departed humans. Several I know actually seem to "download" chunks of information from higher-level beings, which they can then break down and impart to you in words. One psychic I know channels much of the advice she gives from a spirit she believes to be that of Dr. Carl Jung, the famous Swiss psychiatrist.

If these tools or methods are something you feel strongly about, pro or con, keep that in mind when choosing a psychic. A psychic who is very into astrology may speak for a good portion of your reading about planets and their positions in a way that is meaningless—or, alternately, fascinating—to you.

2.

WHEN CHOOSING A PSYCHIC, CHOOSE WISELY.

WHEN LOOKING FOR A GOOD PSYCHIC, don't be lured into a garish storefront or randomly choose someone from an ad. Good psychics often don't advertise; rather, they let their reputations speak for themselves via word of mouth from their satisfied clients, and many psychics rely on that. So, if possible, get a referral from someone who has used the psychic before and been pleased with the results. Ask your friends, family members, or others you may know who are curious about the metaphysical (or "*woo-woo curious*," as I sometimes like to call it) if they have a psychic they really like who also has the skills you're looking for. If you truly don't know anyone interested in things New Age or spiritual, pop into a spiritually oriented bookstore—most towns have one these days—and ask the good people who work there. Chances are someone will know a psychic they trust who fits the bill.

And by all means, Reader, don't trust any psychic who asks for vast sums of money to remove a curse or provide you with an amulet, candle, or blessing to keep you safe, or prevent something disastrous from happening to you. Good psychics know that there are many charlatans out there, preying upon those who are grieving, struggling, or vulnerable in other ways. As they'd be first to assert, if what a psychic tells you scares you, or if you feel threatened or in any way intimidated, run, don't walk, to the nearest exit! (And next time, get a referral.)

And don't forget: If you're happy with the reading you had with your psychic, give them some love and pass their name on to your metaphysically minded or woo-woo curious friends. While some psychics have other "day jobs," those who don't are basically freelancers without benefits, sick pay, or paid vacation. And while some psychics I know have successfully used their skills to pick winning horses and choose lucrative stocks, not all of them have honed those abilities yet, or choose to use their gifts to attempt to do so. So lend a hand when you can. As they say, what goes around comes around.

3.

DO YOUR HOMEWORK BEFORE YOUR READING.

WHEN YOU CONTACT YOUR PSYCHIC to book a session, usually by email or phone, that's the time to ask any questions you may have. It will save time the day of the reading, and often psychics have readings booked back to back. Plus, psychics prefer not to be negotiating the terms of the session when they are preparing to focus, go into trance, or ready their energy in whatever way they do (which varies greatly too) to ensure a good reading.

As mentioned above, ask your potential psychic about their skill set if you're looking for a particular type of information, and their use of any specific systems, tools, etc., if that's something you have preferences about. Find out whether you can ask questions during the reading, or if the psychic just gives you what they get—for example, whatever turns up in the cards, if the psychic uses them. (I've had great readings both ways.) Psychics don't want you to be disappointed if you arrive for your reading only to find out you can't ask the specific questions you had in mind. If you *can* ask questions, prepare a list ahead of time but leave room for spontaneity. You never know where a reading will go and what questions might arise from what's been said. Psychics have pointed out to me that a reading can sometimes be more rewarding if you "go with the flow" of what comes in rather than adhering rigidly to a prepared list.

Ask beforehand if you can record the session or if the psychic may offer a recording as part of the reading—most are happy for you to record it, and some even provide this service! Psychics agree—it's hard for clients to absorb all of what's said the first time they hear it, and sometimes the client's state of mind can affect the way they interpret what's being said. If that's the case, having a recording of your reading allows you to listen to it again, perhaps on a "better day" and with a different perspective. Having the session recorded also enables you to check back on things after some time passes; information that may at first be meaningless to you may become clearer in time. This can be especially true with mediumship readings, where you may want to run precisely what was said, just the way it was said, by other family members or friends who might remember or know things that you didn't, leading you to realize, "Wow! I guess maybe that was Aunt Bernice after all!"

A final suggestion from one psychic I know, for those who may resonate with it, is to raise yourself to a higher vibration before your session. For those not familiar with the term *vibration* used thusly, this refers to the idea that we are all energetic beings, and as such are in a constant state of vibration, at different frequencies (that is, the rate at which the vibration occurs). Methods used to raise one's vibration, or increase one's frequency, include practicing gratitude, listening to or creating music, dancing, being in nature and with animals, and connecting with anything that gives you joy. "Hear your reading from there," this psychic advised, "because it's there, at that higher vibrational location, that you can and will receive the most bang for your buck. Say a prayer, communicate with God, the angels, your own angel—and ask for guidance in your life and in the upcoming session. This is hugely helpful and will bring you to a place of receptivity and peace."

4.

MOST MODERN PSYCHICS *ARE* TECH-SAVVY!

JUST BECAUSE PSYCHIC READING is an age-old profession doesn't mean modern-day psychics don't keep up with the times! Once you get the name of a psychic you're thinking of using, do your homework and check to see if they have a Web site. Not all good psychics necessarily do, but if they *do*, you can often get a reliable sense of them there and sometimes even view videos of them doing their thing. (YouTube and social media platforms are handy for this too.)

Most psychics nowadays work via Zoom, Facetime, or Skype, and they want you to know, it works just as well as an in-person reading! How can this be? Well, there's no need to be physically near the client to get an accurate reading, strange as that may sound. (It's all about picking up on a person's energy . . . and energy knows no bounds! More on that to come.) Some psychics have actually told me that not only can they read just as well over the phone as they do in person, they often give *better* readings by phone! And I have to say, I've had some excellent readings that way.

Why? Apparently, visuals can be distracting. Without a visual image, the psychic may be able to focus in more clearly, and the information received may be more "pure." Also, and this is just my guess based on the phone readings I've had, not being able to see the client may open up the psychic's other senses more. For example, one psychic conducting a phone reading with me could actually feel the slope of my old, tenement-style apartment's warped wooden floors, and smell the burning odor that was emanating from my leaky, rusting radiator! She'd never picked up that kind of sensory detail in my in-person readings with her, and I'd had a good number of them. So if you're not Skype-, Zoom-, or Facetime-savvy, or even if you are, don't dismiss using the good old-fashioned phone!

5.

GOOD PSYCHICS DON'T WANT TO BREAK YOUR BANK.

WHILE MANY FAMOUS PSYCHICS AND MEDIUMS, those who have had their own TV shows or best-selling books, or both, may charge accordingly, good psychics want you to know that you don't have to shell out a fortune to get a high-quality reading. A good psychic is a professional expecting a fair fee for a service well done. Many highly gifted psychics charge very reasonable rates, and some even run sales and specials! Pay is often by the hour, and some will allow you to do a half hour, or even fifteen minutes—usually in person at a psychic fair or in a New Age shop setting—which is not a bad way to try a psychic out. Consider, too, that psychics in different parts of the country may charge less than those in your hometown. If you live in New York City, a psychic in the Midwest may have rates that fit your budget better than those living locally who have higher rents to pay, and a higher cost of living. Since phone or online readings are just as good, or better, what's to stop you?

6.

**DURING YOUR READING,
RELAX AND BE OPEN.**

ONCE YOU'VE VETTED YOUR PSYCHIC via a referral, checked them out on their Web site or YouTube, if possible, or otherwise investigated their work and reputation, relax, open up, and allow them to do their thing. As one psychic I know explained, "If you've done your due diligence—which is important—and you know you're with someone who is gifted, then all you really need to do is to *be open*. A psychic or medium so wants you to have a wonderful and transformative experience, and get from the encounter all that you need. They are one thousand percent on your side, there for you, holding love for you—*big time*!"

Also bear in mind, he added, that "Spirit thinks and knows you are brilliant. And anything that is said or shared in a session is always with the direct intent to walk you to that Truth. So remember that, and start from there—not only in the confines of a session but in life each day: You are brilliant. And you are loved beyond measure—always!"

7.

PSYCHICS DON'T REALLY PREDICT THE FUTURE!

YES, READER, YOU READ THAT RIGHT! While most people think of psychics as *predictors*, every psychic I've interviewed has agreed: It's not really *possible* to accurately predict the future! No prediction will ever be 100 percent correct, and often it will be far less accurate than that. Why? For one thing, they explained, the future is not predestined or written in stone. It's malleable and ever-changing. Earth is a free-will zone, and in any given situation, every person involved can make a myriad of choices, all of which will influence and *co-create* the future outcome you experience. Based on what I've heard from my posse of proven psychics, what they're reading is actually *your energetic field* and is essentially *a snapshot of the possibilities and probabilities present in the field at that moment.*

So don't go into your reading hoping to hear what you want to hear and fall apart if you don't. Realize that what psychics tell you can change . . . and likely WILL change . . . and probably SHOULD change! This is why most psychics—those with integrity, that is—don't like to call themselves *fortune-tellers*. Rather, they prefer terms like *intuitive advisor* or *counselor*. So ask questions and work with your psychic. You *do* have the power to change many things a psychic may see, and a reading can be a tool to help you do just that. (More on this to come as well!)

8.

BETTER READINGS FOCUS ON THE NEAR FUTURE.

ONE PSYCHIC I KNOW SHARED this highly useful nugget with me, and based on what I've just discussed in item 7, it makes perfect sense. The further away the event or person he was trying to "see," chronologically speaking, the less clear it was, *because there were still so many variations of potential outcomes that could occur*. Remember "permutations and combinations" from math class, Reader? If you don't, just think about this: The more time that passes from the time of your reading to the event you're asking about, the more opportunities there are for different things to happen that could influence that event. Again, everyone involved in the situation you're asking about has free will and therefore many choices about what actions they may or may not take. Thus, this psychic explained, if he could see something or someone *very clearly* during a reading, it tended to mean that the person or event he saw was coming *soon*.

This can be a game-changer in terms of what you ask about during a reading. And it might make you want to hold off on having a reading till as close to the event you're asking about as possible, or as close to the date at which you need to make a decision as you can. Again, if you view the reading as a snapshot of the present moment, you want to get as clear a picture as possible, with as many curveballs by all parties involved already having been thrown. Good psychics like to be accurate and helpful, and knowing this can help *you* help *them*.

9.

A GOOD PSYCHIC READING IS NOT A GAME OF BLUFF.

GOOD PSYCHICS ARE NOT AIMING to "put one over on you" during a reading, because they come from a place of honesty and integrity. They *want* you to use your judgment and discernment. As one psychic put it, "Don't check your brain at the door. Ask questions. Listen from your own place of power and wisdom, and feel out what is being shared." That said, you may find yourself, especially in your first reading with a particular psychic, or in your first reading ever, experiencing the desire to "test" the psychic out.

This can be especially tempting with mediums, where we are often extremely passionate about knowing that the experience is "for real," and that the medium is truly contacting our departed loved one, but many people I know do it routinely in all types of psychic readings, in an attempt to prove to themselves that what the reader is getting could only have been gotten through psychic means. Years ago, one friend of mine donned an actual "costume" for an in-person reading with a rather well known psychic, wearing office attire that belied her bohemian artist's lifestyle, and a wedding ring when she was decidedly single. (And yes, Reader, the psychic saw through it all.)

Believe me, I'm not immune to such desires. During my own research, I was often "testing" and "experimenting" to ascertain whether a psychic's abilities were "for real." Early on, I made it a policy never to tell a psychic anything about myself— what kind of work I did, where I lived, whether or not I was married, and so on.
However, over the course of time and many readings, I learned something valuable: While intuition comes

through in many ways, as mentioned earlier, the intuitive impressions that come through for a psychic are very often subject to *interpretation*. Images, or even words, that a psychic picks up—which, we must remember, are coming from a highly unusual source, in a highly unusual way—can often be symbolic, or have multiple meanings.

Here's an example: One well-known psychic told me a story of seeing, during a reading, a client selling several "properties." The client insisted this must be wrong, as he was not in the real estate business and didn't even own his own apartment. As it turned out, the "properties" were *screenplays*—the word is commonly used in the movie industry—as the client realized when, some time after the reading, he simultaneously sold three of them. In this case, when the psychic heard this from the client months later, he was pleased—but frustrated, too, that the client had never revealed the fact that he was a screenwriter. "When the client makes it a guessing game," he told me, referring to this incident, "it not only makes it harder for the psychic, but prevents the reading from progressing as well as it might."

My advice? Work *with* your psychic, not against them. Opening up a bit to your psychic or medium, especially once they've proven themselves and gained your trust, rather than approaching the reading like a poker game between adversaries, may allow the information the psychic receives to be clearer to them, and ultimately to you. Thus, it may also allow for more helpful advice to be given to you, or for further discussions to occur, based on that information, that might be of use or interest.

10.

THERE'S ALWAYS THE POTENTIAL FOR MISINTERPRETATION.

EVEN IF YOU'VE SINCERELY ATTEMPTED to work with your psychic, rather than keeping a poker face, there may be times when the impressions they pick up and the guidance they attempt to give may be lacking in clarity for both of you. Psychics who pick things up visually, for instance, have to interpret what they psychically "see." Case in point, a psychic once warned me to be careful while walking in a dark, narrow space, like an alleyway, as she saw a potential collision with a vehicle there. Nothing terrible, she said, but I should keep my wits about me. Not long after that, the collision did occur, but the dark alleyway was a narrow hallway in my apartment and the vehicle my roommate's Razor scooter sitting on his bedroom floor, which dislocated my pinkie toe. (*Ouch*!) No judgment meant to this gifted psychic, but had she been able to see the scooter itself as part of the picture, that might have helped me be wary of it and make sure it was safely scooted out of harm's way. Alas, what comes in, comes in, and psychics must do the best they can. So, just remember . . . things can get "lost in translation."

There's another potential wrinkle to all this too. One psychic told me that because she picks up on energy, she can at times be picking up on energy in the form of *other people's thoughts*—that is, the people you're asking her about. Once I learned that, I found that other psychics in my posse could actually read a person's thoughts too—though most would define it as *reading a person's energy*—provided the information was something that the client should rightfully know. It's an amazing skill, and has come in handy for me many a time, Reader, especially with my questions about members of the oh-so-quixotic male sex. However, it does have a downside. If the dreamy guy you've been dating all year is *thinking* about popping the question, the psychic may pick up on that, raising your hopes sky-high . . . though in reality McDreamy may never do more than *think about it*! Which, of course, can set you up for some massive frustration and disappointment. So keep that in mind.

11.

EVEN GOOD PSYCHICS SOMETIMES CAN'T GET AN ANSWER.

I'VE EXPERIENCED THIS MYSELF, even with psychics who have astounded me with their accuracy in numerous previous readings. One of them explained it thusly: She said that her guides didn't want to reveal a particular answer just yet; that, for whatever reason, they felt it should not be shared with me at the present time. Also, she said, some things needed to unfold as they would—to be left, for the moment, as a mystery, and were not things I should attempt to control. Given this psychic's great track record over so many readings, I believed her.

Similarly, another psychic with a proven track record told me that her guide didn't want her to give me too many details about a man she saw me meeting because the guide felt I might meet a "double" and mistake that man for him. In essence, her guide was trying to help me avoid some potential heartbreak or difficulty that might occur if he told me too much. It had made me laugh. I'd been known to fixate on details my intuitive friends received about some upcoming man—how many siblings he had, what he'd be wearing when we met, what color car he drove. If anyone appeared in my life who fit even *some* of these descriptors, Reader, I'd start wondering if it was *the guy*. But I'd never thought of the possibility that I could meet a guy who *fit all of the descriptors* and still might not be the guy the psychic had seen!

So don't judge your psychic if they come up blank on a question or two, or tell you something similar to what these psychics told me. There may well be reasons certain things are not revealed to you. If you trust your psychic, trust that their sources may have their reasons "which reason knows not of."

12.

MEDIUMS ARE MIDDLEMEN AND -WOMEN—NOT THE SOURCE!

WHEN IT COMES TO MEDIUMS, it's important to keep an open mind about not only what you'll hear, but *who you'll hear from*. Know that the medium is just that—a "vessel," conduit, or messenger for spirit. While some mediums say they are always able to contact the loved one the client asks for, or in some rare instances a "messenger" sent by that spirit, who comes in their place, others say that who shows up is strictly up to the "dead people" and out of the medium's control. As one medium put it to me, "I can't guarantee who comes in, and I say that at the beginning of each session. It may not be who you want. You may have hated that person. Or you barely knew them. Or they could have died years before you were born. Even though they've been dead for years, believe me, they still know what's happened to you."

According to several mediums I've spoken with, some spirits seem to be naturally better at communicating with those of us here on Earth, and at this level of consciousness, than others. This notion has borne out in my own readings, where, even with different mediums, the same departed loved ones tend to show up again and again, without my ever asking for them. Thus the use, sometimes, as mentioned above, of "messengers." Think of it this way: If chatting with the human realm proves not to be your forte when you've crossed over, you might send your friend Chachi, who's fantastically adept at it, in your place. Alternatively, one spirit may sometimes "escort" another one in. I've had this happen numerous times. It's as if the first spirit is a kind of "way-shower" for the one you've asked to speak to. So yes, spirits on the Other Side may at times need as much help connecting as we do, here on this one!

In any case, don't be too focused, if possible, on hearing from one specific departed individual. Be patient and try to appreciate whoever—or whatever—comes in (I've had departed pets surprise me by showing up too!). Admittedly, that can be hard if you're grieving a recent or even a long-standing loss. But having an accurate and meaningful communication with *anyone* from the spirit world may at least validate for you that mediumship is real, and assure you that your loved one's consciousness still exists.

On a similar note . . .

13.

DON'T ARGUE WITH OR VENT ON YOUR PSYCHIC.

THE PSYCHICS I KNOW AGREE: If you don't like or understand something they pick up in a reading, it's perfectly fine to ask questions about it—bearing in mind that *pausing to listen to what comes next* before doing so may well clarify the information in question. But arguing about the truth of it doesn't help! It's a waste of the psychic's time and energy—and, frankly, your own. As one psychic told me, "Having a sitter [another word for *client*] argue with me makes my trance harder to hold. Also, *the sitter's energy helps focus the energy of the psychic so that the psychic can get the information that the sitter wants*. (Reader, who knew?) When the sitter's energy isn't there, which happens when the sitter argues, and lasts from that point until the end of the session, it's like pulling teeth. You can get some information, but it's difficult to get to the depth required to receive specific details."

For example, he told me, telling a client the truth about a new guy she's met sometimes results in arguments. "'No, he's really nice, he would never cheat or lie to me,' she might say. No matter how hard I then seek other information to show the sitter the error of her ways, she may persist in telling me how wrong I am, as if I'm making it up." Psychics want you to remember that they, like mediums, are also conduits, and not the source. They don't control or govern what comes in. As another psychic once memorably put it: "I'm just the lady at the lunch counter wearing a hairnet and serving it up!"

Also, this last psychic added, what comes in is *in an order of priority* and not necessarily what you *want*, but what you *need*. "Don't shoot the messenger," he added. "Many of us have a terrible habit that seems to be acceptable and it isn't: When we don't like something [we hear], we seem to feel it is OK to behave poorly and blast or hurt others. We, psychics, are not here for your bad behavior or nastiness. Raise yourself up to the Glorious being you are and behave accordingly. If you're having a challenging moment, know that that's fine. Being a mess, being angry, being sad or upset is OK. We've all been there, and are there for you. So . . . be nice to the psychic. They neither need nor want your wrath, and cruelty is unacceptable—always."

Which brings me, Dear Reader, to my next point . . .

14.

REMEMBER, PSYCHICS ARE PEOPLE TOO.

PSYCHICS ARE HUMAN, and they have their good days and bad days, just as you do. Many psychics I've spoken to have admitted to me that giving a reading when they're not feeling physically up to par or are going through a divorce or other emotionally charged situation can definitely influence the quality and accuracy of that reading. Because of this, even good psychics who get many things uncannily right occasionally get a few things decidedly wrong.

One psychic I worked with who had an impeccable accuracy record over a number of years—perhaps the best of all the psychics I worked with—once told me that a house I was inquiring about that was for sale would not sell quickly. In fact, though, it sold within a very few days. She had a similar "miss" with an equally black-and-white question I asked her about in that same reading. As it happened, she was going through an excruciatingly tough time in her personal life. And yes, when that passed, her great accuracy resumed. So when booking your session, you may want to let your psychic know that if they feel they're having an "off" day or are unwell, you'd prefer to postpone the reading to a day when they're at their best. If some "misses" do happen with a psychic you've come to know and trust, understanding this might help you feel less perplexed, and give you pause before writing off a good psychic forever.

Know, too, that as human beings, psychics have their own filters. In other words, remember that a psychic's own emotions, psychology, and life experiences may *color the way they interpret* what they intuitively pick up. Know that they are doing their best. Know that what they receive is subject, to some extent, to associations or even projections they may make. And take what's being said with that in mind.

Plus, as one psychic I spoke to pointed out: "Psychics are people—and a particular person might simply not be a good fit for you, or anybody else, at that time in their own development."

15.

YOUR READING IS A TOOL FOR SHAPING YOUR FUTURE... BUT IT'S UP TO YOU TO USE IT!

ONE PSYCHIC EXPRESSED TO ME another hesitation about making predictions, aside from the ever-changing nature of the future: Knowing what's ahead doesn't usually help people change it. In fact, it may well frighten them, which can actually cause them to feel paralyzed and unable to take action at all. If you don't like what you hear about the current probable outcome of a given situation, ask your psychic if they can advise you as to how you might attempt to change or influence it. Ask if there are any choices you can make, actions you can take, or behaviors you can alter that might affect the situation's outcome. Again, most of the psychics I've interviewed describe themselves as *counselors* or *advisors*—one even calls herself an *intuitive coach*. Their aim is to guide you, and in some cases to help you avoid the probable future toward which you're heading.

That said, one psychic told me of a challenge she has at times faced. Sometimes a client needs to have a conversation with an *attorney* about a problem they're having, but calls a *psychic* instead. "What they're really hoping is that the psychic will soothingly say, 'Don't worry, sweetie, everything will work out. Just surround yourself with white light and pray to your spirit guides.' I call bullshit on that! This kind of person doesn't want to hear any bad news or grapple with a tough issue!"

For example, she told me, an older woman came to her very upset. Her son and his wife had cut her off from seeing their kids, and she wanted to know if she'd be seeing those grandkids in the future. "I told her my psychic feeling was no, and to talk to a lawyer because her state might have grandparents' rights. I said that her son and his wife weren't going to relent on their own, but the minute they saw a lawyer's letter, they would. But she told me she didn't want to sue her son. 'I'm just talking about a letter,' I said. She never contacted a lawyer, but kept calling me. Eventually, I had to cut her off.

"Here's the really crazy part," she went on. "After our initial reading, in which I told her to find out if New York had grandparents' rights and contact a lawyer if so, she happened to chat with a woman in front of her in a grocery-store line *who was going through the same thing*, and who told her that in New York she did have these rights, also providing her with a wealth of related information! My immediate reaction was that the Other Side had set up this serendipitous meeting to help my client. But did she follow up on it? Nope. All she wanted was to pay me to tell her everything would be OK, which I wasn't going to do."

When it comes to *mediums*, I've been told, another, similar issue often arises: Clients may want their departed loved ones to provide them with an ironclad roadmap to get them through whatever tough situation they're facing. That doesn't, of course, always happen. As one medium reminded me, we are here to learn, and the spirits will sometimes—or *often*—let us fall flat on our faces. "Those on the Other Side are not the cavalry, riding in to rescue us," she said. "For instance, a spirit could come through and tell you to get out of your current job *now*, because layoffs are coming. But they're not going to deliver a fabulous new job to your doorstep. It's up to you to get your resume together and start looking!"

As all the psychics I've interviewed see it, readings of any kind are a great *tool* that we can use—*if we actually do what's suggested*!—to heal ourselves and improve our lives. They can help us get answers, achieve results, and create the potential future we want—and avoid the possible future we don't. Think of the Ghost of Christmas Yet to Come in Charles Dickens's *A Christmas Carol*, who showed Scrooge his own "probable future," chock full of sadness and misery, one fateful Christmas Eve night, prompting him to make the necessary changes to create for himself, and those around him (remember Tiny Tim?), a happier life.

AFTERWORD

AND THERE, READER, YOU HAVE THEM—fifteen pearls of wisdom gleaned from my interviews and research with my Dream Team of psychics and mediums. If you're preparing for your first reading, you can now feel confident that you know what to expect and will be far less likely to have post-reading regrets. If you're a veteran with scores of readings under your belt, I trust that there are a few ideas here that you haven't considered before and that will enhance your readings in the future.

If you've enjoyed the insights and anecdotes I've shared here, you'll discover more in my book *Adventures of a Soul: Psychics, Mediums, the Mystical, and Me*. It's the story of how a broken heart and the sudden death of a friend set me off on a quest for answers to life's Big Questions, and how I assembled my Dream Team of psychics and mediums to guide me on a wild expedition into the metaphysical world. It's a tale about life, death, life after death, soul mates and past lives, angels and spirit guides ... with a few life lessons and some laughs along the way. Most of all, it's an account of how the paranormal became my new normal ... and reading it might just make the paranormal *your* new normal too!

Adventures of a Soul: Psychics, Mediums, the Mystical, and Me is now available for purchase both in print and e-book editions from Amazon and other online booksellers. It is also available for order at local bookstores.

For updates about Anne Newgarden, please visit AnneNewgarden.com and sign up for my "Dear Readers" newsletter. You'll also find info on my upcoming events, workshops, book releases, and other news-y stuff, as well as my "Paranormal Is the New Normal" blog, where I'll be posting my latest discoveries for the woo-woo curious that I can't wait to share.

With love, and wishing you your own joyful and exciting explorations ...

Anne

READINGS DIARY

I've found keeping a diary of my readings to be extremely helpful. For each reading, I make a note of the date and the psychic or medium I'm working with. Prior to the reading, I write a list of questions I'm planning to ask—aware that I may well deviate from them, depending on what information comes up in the reading that may spark further inquiry. (It's always good to stay flexible and not to be too wedded to the questions you planned to ask if the reading takes a turn in an unexpected and interesting direction.)

During the reading, I also use my diary to take notes. While I recommend recording your reading if at all possible, having a place to jot down things that may occur to you that are not actually being said (and thus recorded) can be helpful. While most of us are not adept at shorthand and can't write down, word for word, what's being said, taking notes on the most important information coming through is also a good idea, I've found. It can be a godsend if you find out, after recording your reading, that you hit Pause instead of Record, or that there was a technical glitch that rendered your recording unintelligible. (Reader, it's happened to me!)

Please use these diary pages to try out this practice. I trust you'll find it's useful for you too!

ABOUT THE AUTHOR

ANNE NEWGARDEN was born and raised in Staten Island, New York City's "forgotten borough," where her fascination with the metaphysical began, and has been grateful for many years to call Greenwich Village her home. She attended Manhattan's Stuyvesant High School and majored in English at the University of Virginia.

Anne has worked as a writer and editor in the field of children's educational and entertainment media; a copy editor/proofreader in magazine and book publishing; a personal assistant to a celebrated folk musician; a project coordinator in an experimental NYC public school classroom; and a concession-stand manager at an Off-Broadway theater, among other interesting jobs.

Her published works include two pop-up books for grownups with artist Chuck Fischer, a movie tie-in book about Jane Austen, and several essays and articles on various subjects, both woo-woo and non-woo-woo, and for both kids and adults.

Anne loves strong coffee, independent movie theaters, sandpipers, small children, and expanding her consciousness, not exclusively or necessarily in that order, and has always been happiest by the water. She writes and plays, whenever she can, at the Jersey Shore.

www.ingramcontent.com/pod-product-compliance
Lightning Source LLC
Chambersburg PA
CBHW072130070526
44585CB00016B/1613